PASSION TO PROFIT

Diana Richardson-Phillipus

ALL RIGHTS RESERVED. No part of this book or its associated ancillary materials may be reproduced or transmitted in any form or by any means, electronic or mechanical, including photocopying, recording, or by any information storage or retrieval system without permission of publisher.

PUBLISHED BY: DR Global, LLC.

DISCLAIMER AND/OR LEGAL NOTICES

While all attempts have been made to verify information provided in this book and its ancillary materials, neither the author nor publisher assumes responsibility for errors, inaccuracies, or omissions and is not responsible for any monetary loss in any matter. If advice concerning legal, financial, accounting or related matters is needed, the services of a qualified professional should be sought. This book or its associated ancillary materials, including verbal and written training, is not intended for use as a source of legal, financial, or accounting advice. You should be aware of the various laws governing business transactions or other business practices in your state. The information contained in this book is strictly for educational purpose. Therefore, if you wish to apply ideas contained in this book, you are taking full responsibility for your actions. There is no guarantee or promise, expressed or implied, that you will earn any money using the strategies, concepts, techniques, exercises and ideas in the book.

STANDARD EARNINGS AND INCOME DISCLAIMER

With respect to the reliability, accuracy, timeliness, usefulness, adequacy, completeness, and/or suitability of information provided in this book, DR Global, LLC. its partners' associates, affiliates, consultants, and/or presenters make no warranties, guarantees, representations, or claims of any kind. Participants' results will vary depending on many factors. All claims or representations as to income earning are not considered as average earnings. All products and services are for educational and informational purposes only. Check with your accountant, attorney, or professional advisor before acting on this or any information. By continuing with reading this book, you agree that DR Global, LLC. is not responsible for the success or failure of your personal, business, or financial decisions relating to any information.

PRINTED IN THE UNITED STATES OF AMERICA | FIRST EDITION

© All Rights Reserved. Copyright 2022. DR Global, LLC.

TABLE OF CONTENTS

Introduction   7

Passion & Purpose   11

What Makes People Self-Motivated?   12

Lack of Energy or Self-Motivation?   13

Making Decisions   14

The Three Decisions That Will Shape Your Life   16

The NAC Concept of Pain and Pleasure   17

Your Beliefs Have the Power to Create and Destroy   18

Transforming Yourself   20

Motivating Strategies for Taking Action on Your Transformational Decision   22

How Inspirational Quotes Can Motivate You   28

Identify Your Passions and Interests   44

Validate Your Side Hustle	47
Determine What Sets You Apart From Your Competitors	50
Define Your Goals	53
Create Milestones	56
Determine How You Will Sell	59
Start Selling	62
Market Yourself	64
Get Feedback From Your Customers	67
Provide Amazing Experiences For Your Customers	69
Build Sustainable Cash Flow	72
Side Hustle Your Way To Freedom	75
DAILY AFFIRMATIONS AND SELF REFLECTION TOOLS	**77**
Blessings are real.	78
I am full of life.	80
I choose my state of being.	82
I choose my state of being.	84
My life journey brings me joy.	86
Each day brings joy, fulfillment, and happiness.	88
I am living my life fully.	90

I choose to be content.	92
I live in a land of liberty.	94
Sharing makes me happy.	96
Each day I grow more energetic and vital.	98
I am living my perfect life now.	100
I choose to smile and enjoy life to the fullest.	102
I receive what I need.	104
Simple living makes me happy.	106
Each day is a blessing and a gift that I refuse to waste.	108
I am peaceful, calm, and contented.	110
I feel safe and loved.	112
I return to happiness.	114
This is exactly where I am supposed to be.	116
Exploring the world is exciting.	118
I am so happy.	120
I find happiness in the present.	122
I see all the blessings around me.	124
Today is a day of happiness and peace for me.	126
Happiness heals me.	128
I find the sweetness in life.	130

PASSION TO PROFIT

I start each day feeling happy and enthusiastic. 132

Today is an amazing day. 134

Happiness is a habit. 136

I fulfill my responsibilities with joy. 138

INTRODUCTION

There is no being or thing that exists outside its relevance or purpose. Creativity and productivity show that there is a reason for creation. We handle material and physical things, and the very notion of their existence reflects the purpose behind their being. It is also acknowledged that as humans, we long for fulfillment in different aspects of our lives. This desire stems from the objective or goals we set out to achieve.

It is, therefore, safe to say that man has a purpose. Man is driven by reason. There's a reason and motive behind every word and action of man. For some people, it is the desire to be heard; for some, it is the desire to achieve their aspirations. Notwithstanding how enormous or minute one's purpose may be, personal fulfillment comes from accomplishing these desires.

It is important that you discover your purpose, but it is not as vital as being passionate about it. Passion is the fuel that keeps your vision going until it is achieved. Passion energizes your focus on the goal. It keeps you determined, resilient, and unwavering. Simply put, without passion, the journey to fulfilling purpose will be a tortoise-paced one. However, because your passion keeps you on track, you are not distracted from your pursuit.

Hence, dealing with life and living life to the uttermost has its dependency on purpose and passion. Without purpose, your zeal will be based on ignorance and confusion. This will yield futile efforts and a merry-go-round journeying. With no purpose, there won't be a need for zeal. Also, without enthusiasm, purpose will be as dead as a withered plant.

The symbiotic relationship between these two is an essential key to your success. Therefore, laying this foundation is paramount. When you see the connection between the two, it will be easy for you to identify where to exert your energy. To keep your dreams, hopes, aspirations, and goals alive, you must consistently fuel them with passion. As a result, your morale concerning these things remains high regardless of the challenges that you may encounter.

By understanding this, you will realize that it takes more than plans and strategies to stay afloat, especially in a world that is full of competition and limiting factors. Planning or strategizing is not out of the curriculum, but it is a subsidiary. Planning helps you to recognize your opportunities and scale the obstacles. But passion helps you to be dogged, with or without challenge. By this, you have the acuity and diligence required in accomplishing your goals.

Now, you owe yourself the duty to remain zealous and focus on your purpose. With this, you will draw strength and determination. Look introspectively, search within you and acknowledge if you are among those who long to be fulfilled. If you discover that you are among them, then you are doing the right thing by reading this book.

I will advise that you absorb and imbibe the apt nuggets written on the leaves of this book. Let it sink in and then radically change your life as you put into action what you learn.

WANTING SOMETHING IS NOT ENOUGH. YOU MUST HUNGER IN ORDER TO OVERCOME THE OBSTACLES THAT WILL INVARIABLY COME YOUR WAY.

– *LES BROWN*

PASSION & PURPOSE

All of us have dreams of a better life, but somewhere along our journey, these dreams can get buried. When the chaos of everyday life takes over, we may even begin to believe that we're not capable of achieving our goals! *Nothing* could be further from the truth.

This little book will show you how to use the power of your mind to motivate yourself to pursue your goals to fulfillment, regardless of the challenges life throws your way. It will also give you expert advice on staying motivated throughout your life.

Many of the techniques and suggestions are based on those taught by Anthony Robbins, who rose from the status of janitor to become one of the most successful self-help and inspirational authors in the world. One day he was sitting in his bachelor pad, overweight and aimless, and a year later, he was living in his own castle!

What turned Mr. Robbins' life around? Read on to discover these techniques and how you, too, can take advantage of these same principles and more to gain the motivation to attain the life you desire.

WHAT MAKES PEOPLE SELF-MOTIVATED?

elf-motivated people are passionate about their interests and beliefs. For instance, they could be health enthusiasts who understand why health is crucial to their success. Because they believe this, they do everything they can to be healthy.

Those who are self-motivated are also advocates of discipline. Without this mind set, it's not possible to follow a regular routine of exercise, a healthy diet, or do anything else which requires daily effort, like working toward the achievement of your goals.

LACK OF ENERGY OR SELF-MOTIVATION?

It's possible to mistake a lack of energy for an absence of self-motivation. If you feel too fatigued to act in a motivated way, you may be experiencing challenges that go deeper than self-motivation.

You might be fighting feelings of excess stress, depression, or low self-esteem. These mental challenges compromise your desire to accomplish your goals. You might have a physical reason for your lack of motivation – low energy caused by poor nutrition, lack of exercise, or even not enough sleep.

Adding nutritious foods and vitamin supplements to your diet, exercising, and acquiring good sleep habits can go a long way towards increasing your energy. Daily meditation can reduce stress, promote feelings of wellbeing, raise your self-esteem, and increase your energy.

If you find yourself seriously lacking the energy to work towards the fulfillment of your dreams, check with your doctor or other health professional for a regimen that can increase your energy.

MAKING DECISIONS

According to Anthony Robbins, *our destiny is shaped in the very moment of decision making.* A "true decision," says Robbins, "entails a commitment to achievement." He advises that no matter what happens, you should stick by these decisions and learn from them whether they work or not. If they don't work, change your approach until they do. Be flexible and look for alternate routes.

Follow these strategies to make effective decisions that give you the commitment to take positive action toward the life you seek:

1. **Avoid making excuses.** Excuses for *not* making decisions or *not* being able to reach your goals lets you blame your lethargy and aimlessness on the challenges you face in life. Too many others blame past events in their lives for their misery. Don't let this be you!

   » *Seek ways to overcome your challenges* and those de-motivating blame games will become a thing of the past. Taking action to overcome challenges gives you a new way to continue moving forward toward what's important to you and it's extremely motivating!

2. **Be clear about your decisions.** For example, saying that you'd like to quit drinking alcohol is not a "true decision" because it doesn't entail a commitment to achievement. When you make a true decision, you'll decide that you'll never drink alcohol again.

» ***A clear decision with a commitment to achievement makes you feel empowered and relieved.***

How do you know that you've made a "true decision?" If *action* flows from your decision, you can be sure you've made a true decision. If it doesn't, you haven't really decided. Once you act on your decision, you'll set into motion a new cause and effect cycle that will create your new life.

Make quick decisions and make many. Avoid spending ages agonizing over your decision. Instead, decide quickly or the fire in your belly will go out.

Keep making decisions and enjoy making them. You'll be filled with energy and your life will be exciting. Remember, every little decision you make can change the direction of your life the very moment you decide.

THE THREE DECISIONS THAT WILL SHAPE YOUR LIFE

1. **Decide what your primary focus is for each moment of your life.** This will influence your feelings, thoughts, and actions.

2. **Decide how your situations affect you.** Cut through the chaos and pause to answer this question: How does this situation affect my present and future?

3. **Decide what you should do** now. This is a most important decision. Don't be bothered by what others are doing and don't be carried away by what's happening around you. If you do, you're allowing your environment to direct your decision.

THE NAC CONCEPT OF PAIN AND PLEASURE

N AC, or Neuro Associative Conditioning, is based on the pain and pleasure principle. Basically, this technique requires you to associate pain with the things you want to avoid and pleasure with the things you want. As a result, the unconscious mind takes over and conditions you for success.

You can either allow pain and pleasure to control you, or you can use them as tools with which to control your life. The way you react to pain and pleasure determine your actions.

So how do you use this technique? Here's an example: You can replace the pain of eating soybeans with the pleasure of being healthier. You can do this by visualizing yourself as fitter and healthier whenever you eat soybeans.

YOUR BELIEFS HAVE THE POWER TO CREATE AND DESTROY

Your beliefs have plenty to do with your motivation. If you believe that being overweight is in your genes, you can't hope to lose weight even if you exercise. If you believe in your capabilities, you can be a hero. If you believe you're a failure, you'll fail.

You can use the pain and pleasure principle to change your negative beliefs:

1. **Look deep within to discover the unconscious beliefs you harbor.** Perhaps you believe that all marriages are destined to fail, automobile accidents are waiting to happen, or the efforts of just one individual can't make a significant difference to the world. These types of beliefs are negative and can severely limit your commitment to the success you deserve.

2. **Think of the effect that your negative beliefs have on you.** Is it an obstacle to the life you want? Feel the pain.

Then replace it with a positive belief that will help you succeed. Visualize and feel this success.

3. **Replace your negative beliefs with positive ones by questioning and re-examining your belief structure,** thus building up evidence to support your new positive beliefs. For instance, you can think of individuals who *have* made a difference to the world without help from anyone else.

   » For example, when Mother Teresa decided to leave the convent and go out into the slums to help the poor, she was alone. But not for long. Her commitment to positive action influenced not only those she helped, but eventually, people all over the world.

TRANSFORMING YOURSELF

············●●●●●●●●············

The change you seek could be behavioral or attitudinal and requires some amount of re-programming, but as Mark Twain said: "There is nothing training cannot do. Nothing is above its reach. It can turn bad morals into good. It can destroy bad principles and recreate good ones. It can lift men to angel ship."

Robbins points out that change happens in an instant. What takes time is getting to this point. For change to happen, you need to believe that you *can* change this very instant, and that *you* are the one responsible for your own transformation. You can't expect others to change you, nor can you blame them if you fail to change.

Here are the steps Robbins suggests:

1. **Decide what you** really **want to change in your life.** Ask yourself what's preventing you from change. Remember not to focus on what you don't want, but on what you *do* want. Also, ensure you're not linking pain to making the change, as this can lead to failure since your subconscious mind will want to avoid pain, keeping you from succeeding in the change.

2. **Your desire to change should be urgent.** Associate pain with not changing *now* and pleasure with changing *now*.

3. **Questions That Induce Pain.** Feel the pain when you answer these questions:
   » What will this cost me if I don't change?
   » What has it already cost me physically, spiritually, mentally, career-wise, and in my relationships?
   » How has it affected my family and friends?

4. **Pleasure Associating Questions.** Feel the pleasure intensely as you answer these questions:
   » If I transform myself, how will it make me feel about myself?
   » What will this change help me accomplish?
   » How will this change make my family and friends feel?

MOTIVATING STRATEGIES FOR TAKING ACTION ON YOUR TRANSFORMATIONAL DECISION

1. **Do your research.** Finding out more about your subject will generate interest and motivation. For example, if you want to learn how to play the guitar, subscribe to a good magazine on the subject.

   » For example, look at Frank's story: Frank didn't know how interesting gardening could be until he bought himself a beautiful book on gardening. Now it's hard to tear him away from his flowers.

2. **Reward yourself as you progress.** Celebrate your little successes on the way. This will also bring you motivation to continue succeeding.

   » For instance, if you make the "true decision" to lose weight, you will naturally act on it by pushing the plate away. You'll be able to do this by associating the action with the pleasure of being fitter and healthier. Each time you push the plate away, reward yourself with a non-edible treat like a telephone call to a supportive friend.

3. **Join a community.** Working together with others who share your goals and ideals will allow you to learn from their mistakes and successes. It can keep the fires burning and get you back on track if you go astray.

4. **Befriend motivated people.** Our friends are a powerful influence on our lives. Therefore, we must choose them with care. Make friends with those you admire and look up to. They'll support you and encourage you on your quest for a better life. Plus, they're likely to have the good habits of motivated people. Together you could move mountains!

5. **Seek feedback.** If you blog about your big and little successes, you'll probably get lots of encouragement. Just writing the blog will help to keep you going. It will inspire others and, in turn, motivate you.

6. **Relive past successes.** If you study high achievers, you'll notice that they have a positive self-image. They focus on their past successes in order to make them happen again. You, too, can remember and visualize how good a past success made you feel. Do this every morning. Your brain will create new neural pathways and help you replicate this state of success.

7. **Keep your target in sight.** Keeping your target firmly in your mind will reflect in your body language. Focus on

the pleasures and rewards in store and you'll get more of what you focus on.

8. **Be tenacious.** Act towards the attainment of your target every day. Don't let a day go by without taking action, even in a small way, to reach your goal.

9. **Read inspirational material.** Read inspirational stories about others who have achieved their goals against all odds. These could be well known people or ordinary people who have, as Robbins would put it, "awakened the giant within." If you can't manage the time to read, you could listen to motivational recordings while driving to work.

10. **Visualize the outcomes repeatedly.** Although this technique takes a bit of practice, it's one of the most powerful ways to stay motivated. Visualize the outcome of your goals.

    » How does visualization work? The brain cannot tell something vividly imagined from reality. If you feed a vivid picture into your brain repeatedly, it will begin to manifest it as reality.

11. **Have a goal.** Motivation doesn't exist in a vacuum. It's always tied to a goal. Ensure you have clear goals.

12. **Write down your goals.** According to research, people who write down their goals are far more likely to remain motivated and achieve their goals than those who merely make mental lists. To ensure that you always remember your goals, you could write them down where you can readily see them.

> For example, Melanie, whose goal is enlightenment, has written on the wall above her desk where she spends a large part of her day the four attitudes that will help her to get there: "Stillness, Cheerfulness, Humility, and Innocence." She checks herself throughout the day against these criteria.

13. **Give yourself a spiritual goal or noble cause.** Give yourself a worthy cause such as donating money for cancer research or helping others better their lives. Seeing how you affect the lives of those less fortunate will keep you motivated. Your faith in your spiritual path will motivate you to act in the most positive ways to bring about your desired life.

* For example, Melanie's spiritual goal of enlightenment leads her to these positive actions:

    > She'll stay healthy so she can assist her spiritual mentors and community.

    > Even in her profession as a writer, she will invariably spread the message of oneness and compassion.

    > She is vegetarian because she does not want to cause suffering.

    > She has given up cigarettes because she believes it will destroy not just her health, but also her wisdom.

    > The generosity and unselfishness she portray to her spiritual community reflects in her dealings with the world.

14. **Be health conscious.** Energy and good health help you stay motivated all day and every day. You should get enough sleep, eat healthily, and exercise regularly. Then taking action towards your goals every day will be much easier.

15. **Know your "peak hours."** All of us have certain times of the day when we feel most energetic and creative. Find out your "peak hours." Are you a morning, afternoon, or evening person? Once you know your most productive time, you can do the tasks that require the most energy during these periods.

16. **Don't look for perfection.** Many a perfectionist gives up on a task before he's even begun, because he's afraid of not being able to do a perfect job. This can lead to procrastination. A good writer, for instance, accepts the fact that he will probably write several drafts before he perfects a piece of writing, and he enjoys it as part of the writing process.

17. **Do the harder task first.** This can work really well. For example, if you have a bunch of articles to write, tackle the toughest first. After that, writing the rest will be easier and you can keep the motivation going.

18. **Practice spiritual awareness.** When you're spiritually aware, you'll do every little task with love and complete awareness, focusing on the task at hand. There will be nothing else in the world for you at the time. Just you and the task. There will be no future, no past, only the present. You'll dwell completely in the moment.

» So how will this awareness come about? It'll be easy if you realize that every trivial task you do is meant for your spiritual evolution. You've encountered the task because it's necessary for your growth. You can do the task with acceptance and appreciation. This positive belief is worth nurturing.

» For instance, when Rita goes for her early morning walk, she's intensely aware of the changes in her body and mind. She notices the trees and flowers, the sky, and the houses she walks by. She isn't thinking about what to cook for lunch or her new dress.

19. Use self-affirmation techniques. Self-affirmation, also known as autosuggestion, is a technique for creating positive changes. It's based on the belief that if you tell yourself something long enough, you'll eventually believe it. Self-affirmations can help you create a new reality, attract the things you want, relax you, and make you healthier.

» When you keep saying something to yourself, you declare it to your brain and the universe. Your brain thinks it's real and the universe works to manifest it. This is a tried and tested NLP (Neuro Linguistic Programming) technique.

» One popular, effective affirmation is "Every day in every way I'm getting better and better." This affirmation has even helped people heal from physical ailments. Note how it's positive (focuses on what you do want rather than what you don't want), personal (uses the word "I"), and in the present tense.

HOW INSPIRATIONAL QUOTES CAN MOTIVATE YOU

Affirmations are a great way to start your day. Closely related to self-affirmations are inspirational quotes. Someone else's idea may resonate with your beliefs and inspire you to keep going, even when the chips are down. Sometimes these sayings can remind you of an important concept that motivates you to take action.

Here's an inspiring quotation for every day of the week:

"EIGHTY PERCENT OF SUCCESS IS SHOWING UP."

– *WOODY ALLEN*

Chances are you know people who keep talking about the wonderful things they want to do, but never get around to doing. They're just not motivated. It's not enough to plan and dream. We must begin with action, even the smallest of actions. This will set the ball rolling and will eventually lead to that big goal.

Woody Allen himself is so self-motivated that he finds the concept of awards "silly." He says, "I cannot abide by the judgment of other people, because if you accept it when they say you deserve an award, then you have to accept it when they say you don't." Winning the Oscar for *Annie Hall* didn't mean anything to him.

"WE WILL EITHER FIND A WAY OR MAKE ONE."

– HANNIBAL

These are the words of a highly self-motivated man feared by Rome for his military genius. And it all began when Hannibal was only nine years old. His father asked him to swear that he would fight their enemy, Rome, when he grew up. Hannibal remembered the promise he made his father and became one of the most brilliant military generals the world has ever seen.

What motivated Hannibal? Love for his father and love for his land, Carthage. Making a promise to someone is definitely one way to stay motivated!

"I HAVE NOT FAILED. I'VE JUST FOUND 700 WAYS THAT WON'T WORK."

– THOMAS A. EDISON

Thomas Edison had very little formal education and was a great believer in self-improvement. Whatever he knew was taught to him by his mother and his own efforts. When his first patented invention, an electric vote recorder, proved a commercial failure, he didn't give up.

You could say that his mother was his motivator. Of her, he said in later years: "My mother was the making of me. She was so true, so sure of me, and I felt I had someone to live for, someone I must not disappoint."

When he was twelve, he lost almost all his hearing, but rather than perceive it as a drawback, he felt it helped him to concentrate on his experiments. Then came the tin foil phonograph, which brought him international fame, followed by the incandescent light bulb which had taken him one and a half years to perfect.

When Edison was asked in an interview how it felt to fail 700 times in his attempts to create the light bulb, he answered: "I have not failed 700 times. I have not failed once. I have succeeded in proving that those 700 ways will not work. When I have eliminated the ways that will not work, I'll find the way that will."

You too can learn from your mistakes. They're not a waste of time as long as you use them to avoid further mistakes. Success comes by trial and error. Keep a journal of your progress. Write down what you did towards realizing your goal every day, even if it's something small. Writing things down will bring clarity to your efforts.

"WE ARE WHAT WE THINK. ALL THAT WE ARE ARISES. WITH OUR THOUGHTS, WE MAKE OUR WORLD."

– THE BUDDHA

You probably know that The Buddha is the ultimate example of self-motivation. As Prince Siddhartha Gautama, he spent the first 30 years of his life coddled and spoiled by his father. He was shielded from all negativity and saw only the beautiful. But he soon tired of pleasures and ventured out of the palace.

The suffering he encountered – old age, sickness and death, made him renounce everything. His goal was to find solutions to these inevitabilities of human existence. Imagine how tough life alone and impoverished would have been for one who had known no hardship! Yet he found what he was looking for and his insights continue to illuminate the minds and hearts of spiritual seekers across the world.

Every action is preceded by a thought. If it's positive, it creates a positive reality; if negative, misfortune. Every action creates a reaction. It's up to you to create the reactions you desire. If you tell yourself you're no good, or that you can't achieve your goals, you're not going to be a success. However, telling yourself how good you are and having faith in yourself can make you a hero.

"SUCCESS IS NOT FINAL,
FAILURE IS NOT FATAL:
IT IS THE COURAGE TO
CONTINUE THAT COUNTS."

– SIR WINSTON CHURCHILL

As a child, Churchill was neglected by his parents and demeaned by other kids. The only affection he had came from his nurse, Mrs. Everest. This is the background which made him want to prove his worth to the world, and as a statesman, orator and journalist, he lives on.

As a successful person, you know that there's always another hill to climb. Never rest on your laurels or get discouraged when obstacles turn up, for when you climb that hill, you discover rewards at the top.

"GOD DOESN'T REQUIRE US TO SUCCEED; HE ONLY REQUIRES THAT YOU TRY."

– MOTHER TERESA

The suffering and poverty Mother Teresa encountered outside the walls of her convent in Calcutta prompted her to leave that secure place to work in the slums. She had no funds, but she had love and a fierce determination. So moving was her compassion, many people joined her in her efforts and the funds began to flow in.

She won the Nobel Peace Prize, and was happy because she could invest the money she won into her work of love. She even cancelled the dinner they were to host for her on the occasion so she could use the money for the poor. Her focus was unwavering.

"ALL MISFORTUNE IS BUT A STEPPINGSTONE TO FORTUNE."

– HENRY DAVID THOREAU

Thoreau was passionate about the joys and healing power of solitude and nature. He dreamed of living a quiet life in the woods, and he did. He was never rich, but no one could say he was poor, because his attitude was not that of the impoverished. So what was the "fortune" he alluded to? Clearly, he meant *inner* riches.

Now that you have the most powerful keys to self-motivation in your hands, it's time to forge ahead and achieve your dreams – starting from this moment!

"BELIEVE IN YOUR DREAMS NO MATTER HOW IMPOSSIBLE THEY SEEM

-WALT DISNEY

IDENTIFY YOUR PASSIONS AND INTERESTS

············●●●●●●············

So how do you identify *what* your side hustle should be? How do you know what you should give your time to? How can you determine the best activities to focus on?

You start by identifying the things you're most passionate about and interested in.

See, a side hustle is the intersection of passion and profit. In other words, it's all about taking the things you love and are good at and turning them into a profitable gig.

So, the first step is to identify what you love to do AND are good at doing.

Both elements are required. If you want your side hustle to be sustainable, you must love doing it. If you don't, you'll burn out quickly. When hard work and sacrifices are needed, you won't want to. A successful side hustle involves an activity that you love doing.

You must also be *good* at your side hustle. In other words, you must have the necessary skill set to make it a reality. If you're not good at creating your product or performing your service, others simply won't want to pay you for it.

Ask yourself these questions:

What do you absolutely love doing?

What have people told you that you're good at?

What do you lose track of time doing?

What valuable skills do you have that people would pay for?

What needs can you meet?

These questions will help you find the intersection of passion and profit. They'll help you determine both your skillset and what you love. When these two things combine, you have a viable side hustle.

There is a psychological concept called "flow." It's when you find yourself so immersed in an activity that you lose all track of time and are simply focused on what's in front of you. Your mind isn't distracted at all. Rather, you simply "flow" with your activity.

When do you find yourself in the "flow" of things? Pay attention to these moments. It's these activities that could turn into viable side hustles.

THE BIGGEST ADVENTURE YOU CAN TAKE IS TO LIVE THE LIFE OF YOUR DREAMS.

- OPRAH WINFREY

VALIDATE YOUR SIDE HUSTLE

.... ● ● ● ● ● ● ●............

Once you've determined what you think your side hustle should be, it's important to validate it. In other words, be able to demonstrate that people will really pay you for what you offer them. Determine if there's a "market need" for the product or services that you will offer.

After all, it won't do you any good to start your side hustle, only to discover that no one actually wants what you're offering. You'll end up spending hours and hours on things that won't generate any extra income. You'll also become discouraged and probably want to give up.

Therefore, it's essential to ensure that people will want what you have to offer, even if it's just a few people.

So how can you do that? Where can you find an audience on which to test out your idea?

Some simple ideas include:

Ask your friends on social media if they would be interested in what you have to offer.

If you have an email list, send out a poll to them, asking who would be interested in what you're going to offer.

Create a sign-up list where people can get more information. If numerous people sign up, it's a sign that your idea has legs.

Offer to let people pre-purchase your offer. If a number of people purchase from you, you know that you're onto something good.

Your goal is to avoid wasting time on ideas that won't get any traction. If your polls, emails, and sign-up list aren't getting much of a response, it may be time to move on to a different side hustle.

It's really important that you not get discouraged at this point. **If you can't get any traction on your side hustle, that doesn't mean you have to give it up altogether.** It simply means you may not be able to make a sustainable income from it. Or, you may simply need to adjust your approach to your product.

There are dozens of ways to make money, and you can certainly find a side hustle that allows you to do what you love.

DREAMS COME TRUE.
WITHOUT THAT
POSSIBILITY, NATURE
WOULD NOT INCITE US TO
HAVE THEM.

-JOHN UPDIKE

DETERMINE WHAT SETS YOU APART FROM YOUR COMPETITORS

Unless you're building something completely new and revolutionary, you're going to be competing against others. Whether you're selling a widget or offering coaching services, there are going to be others against whom you're competing for business.

If you're going to succeed with your side hustle, you need to find a way to differentiate yourself from your competitors. In other words, figure out how you're going to stand out from the crowd. How you're going to attract customers. How your offer is different from what others are offering.

How can you differentiate yourself from your competitors? **There are numerous ways, including:**

- Better quality products or services
- Better customer service
- Faster delivery

Less expensive products or services

Aggressive sales tactics

Higher or lower profit margins

A noble cause that you support with profits from your product

For example, let's say you're selling soap online. You could create a unique soap that is better quality than most other soap out there. Because your soap is better quality, you can sell it for a higher price and make higher profit margins.

Or you could sell your soap at a discount and sell a higher volume of soap. Or you could create an aggressive online marketing campaign where you're trying to get your soap in front of more eyeballs than anyone else.

If you don't find a way to differentiate yourself from your competitors, there's no reason that customers should purchase from you. You absolutely must find a way to stand out in the crowd.

COMMITMENT LEADS TO ACTION. ACTION BRINGS YOUR DREAM CLOSER.

- MARCIA WIEDER

DEFINE YOUR GOALS

Once you've determined what your side hustle will be, have validated that idea, and determined how you'll stand out from the crowd, it's time to define your overall goals. Defining clear goals will help you know what steps you need to take in order to turn your hustle into a reality.

Consider laying out a set of goals that sequentially follow one another.

For example, if you're going to sell products on eBay, your first goal may be to create an eBay account. Your second goal may be to research the products that sell best on eBay. Your third goal may be to source the products to sell and your fourth goal may be to list those products.

When setting your goals, ensure that they are realistic. Your goal is to get traction, not reach your end goal right off the bat. Setting a goal of selling 1,000 bars of soap is a great goal, but there are probably a dozen smaller goals that need to be achieved before you can reach your final goal.

Each goal should be realistic and achievable. If your goals aren't realistic, you'll again find yourself getting discouraged when you don't meet those goals. The more discouraged you get, the more inclined you'll be to give up your side hustle.

So what are some small goals you can set that will give you traction on your hustle? These small goals should all contribute to your big, overall goal.

Do you need to…

Research your market?

Research the desires of your ideal customer?

Create a website?

Send out an email to your list, letting them know about your offer?

Start taking small steps that will lead you to your overall goal. Try to set goals that will move you forward on a daily, weekly, and monthly basis.

THE ONLY BOUNDARIES FOR ME ARE THOSE I PLACE ON MYSELF.

- SHELLY WU

CREATE MILESTONES

One of the great temptations with a side hustle is to put off actually launching. You can get so caught up in trying to make things perfect that you never actually get your side hustle off the ground.

Eventually, you just need to get started. Yes, you need to reach the small goals that will lead you to your big goal, but eventually, you just need to get your idea out into the wild and evaluate the response.

Side hustles are iterative. In other words, you launch, refine, fix problems, and then keep going. With each iteration, your side hustle gets better and better. The more iterations you do, the more highly refined your hustle becomes and the more revenue you generate.

In order to launch, set milestones that will force you to take action. Setting milestones for yourself will ensure that you actually take action and don't delay. Each milestone should be tied directly to a date.

For example, let's say you're launching a coaching program. Your first milestone might be to create your website within the next month. Your next milestone might be to send out an email to all the potential clients you know. Your third milestone might be to advertise your coaching practice on Facebook.

Think of it this way: **Milestones equal movement.** When you set milestones for yourself, it forces you to move forward and prevents you from trying to get everything perfect.

Like your goals, your milestones should also be realistic and achievable. For example, it's probably not realistic to think that you can get a website designed in a day (unless you're an amazing web designer). Give yourself a reasonable amount of time to achieve your milestone.

The more you reach your milestones, the more encouraged you'll be about your side hustle. The more encouraged you are, the more you'll want to reach more milestones, which will keep your project moving at a rapid pace. Avoid making excuses when it comes to meeting your milestones. Hold yourself to deadlines, and if you need to get friends to hold you accountable, don't hesitate to do that.

FIRST SAY TO YOURSELF WHAT YOU WOULD BE; AND THEN DO WHAT YOU HAVE TO DO.

- EPICTETUS

DETERMINE HOW YOU WILL SELL

Before you can launch your side hustle, you'll need to determine *how* you're going to sell your product or service.

Thankfully, there are dozens of ways to sell products and services, such as:

You can always sell in person.

If you're selling a product, you can take it to trade shows and markets.

You could even go from door to door if you have the courage.

You can sell directly to your friends or host parties where you show off your product.

You can meet one-on-one with potential customers and tell them about the benefits of the service you offer.

You can also sell just about any product or service online as well.

For example, if your product is crafty (like soap), artisan, or vintage you can sell on Etsy.

If you're getting products from thrift shops, you can sell them on eBay or Poshmark.

If you're trying to break into the freelance world, you can find jobs in dozens of industries on websites like Upwork, Fiverr, or Thumbtack.

If you're selling eBooks, you can list them on Amazon.

If you're promoting a course you've created, you can sell it through Kajabi, Teachable, Udemy, or Thinkific.

If you're a handyman, you can find hundreds of jobs on Task-Rabbit.

If you're a coach, you can use Tailored.coach to connect with your clients.

And, of course, you can build your own website - your business' home on the web.

No matter what you're selling, there is an online platform to sell it. A simple way to find the platform that's best for you is to Google "Sell [PRODUCT/SERVICE] online". This will bring up dozens of results and allow you to find the best place to sell your product or service.

I HAVE ACCEPTED FEAR AS A PART OF LIFE - SPECIFICALLY THE FEAR OF CHANGE.

I HAVE GONE AHEAD DESPITE THE POUNDING IN THE HEART THAT SAYS: TURN BACK.

- ERICA JONG

START SELLING

This point is short and sweet. Once you've done the initial work up front, you simply need to get started.

Your side hustle will *not* be perfect when you first launch it. You'll make mistakes. You may have trouble landing your first customers. Regardless, at some point, you must launch your side hustle if you want to make any money from it.

As noted above, building a successful side hustle involves a lot of tweaking, refining, and making changes on the fly. If you try to get everything perfect before you launch, you'll never get started.

In the initial launch phase, it may take some time for you to gain significant traction. You'll have to work hard to promote yourself. But it's worth the work. If your side hustle is valuable, people will eventually buy into it.

Avoid getting discouraged if you don't have massive success right off the bat. Keep working, refining, promoting, and selling. Eventually, you'll hit on the right combination and the customers will start coming.

FIGURE OUT WHAT YOUR PURPOSE IS IN LIFE, WHAT YOU REALLY AND TRULY WANT TO DO WITH YOUR TIME AND YOUR LIFE; THEN BE WILLING TO SACRIFICE EVERYTHING AND THEN SOME TO ACHIEVE IT.

- QUINTINA RAGNACCI

MARKET YOURSELF

To make your side hustle as successful as possible, it's essential to consistently market yourself. You'll need to promote your hustle, so it gets in front of as many people as possible.

Don't be modest on this point. If you truly believe in what you're doing, then go for it with all your might. Market yourself hard and relentlessly.

What are some effective ways to market your side hustle?

Ask your friends and family to spread the word.

Hand out flyers telling others about what you offer.

Give out free samples (if you're selling a product).

Tell people about it on social media.

Build an email list and regularly promote your product or service to the list.

Start a blog and consistently talk about pain points your customers feel.

Create a YouTube channel specifically dedicated to giving loads of value to potential customers.

Start a podcast in which you talk about elements of your industry and business.

Appear as a guest on other's podcasts.

Do webinars where you teach valuable lessons and then promote your product or service at the end.

Use paid advertising to drive people to your website.

Consistently apply for jobs on the platforms mentioned above.

Generally speaking, the more value you can give potential customers for *free*, the more likely they are to pay for your product or services.

For example, let's say you're a health and fitness coach. You could create a YouTube channel in which you teach people exercises and workout routines. This is giving free value to people.

The more you do this, the more people will see that you're an expert in your field and the more they'll want to hire you as their health and fitness coach.

Again, don't be afraid to market yourself. You've put in hours of hard work to get to this point. You've created a product or service that you truly believe in. You know that you truly can help people and really want to make a difference in the world.

So, try to get yourself in front of as many people as possible. Don't worry about what others will think. If you want to succeed with your side hustle, you must market yourself constantly.

VISION WITHOUT ACTION IS MERELY A DREAM. ACTION WITHOUT VISION JUST PASSES THE TIME. VISION WITH ACTION CAN CHANGE THE WORLD.

-JOEL BARKER

GET FEEDBACK FROM YOUR CUSTOMERS

········•••••••·•·•••••·······

After you've launched, keep improving. If you want to achieve the kind of success that will change your life, you need to constantly better the product or service that you're offering.

After all, some people will buy an okay product or service. A LOT of people will buy an outstanding product or service.

This is where customer feedback is invaluable. Your customers can honestly tell you what is and what isn't working. They can help you see past your blind spots and identify areas for change that you never would have seen on your own.

So, ask your customers these important questions:

What do they like about your product or service?

What features do they find most valuable and which ones could use improvement?

How has your product or service benefited them and what benefits would they still like to see?

Which pain points could you more effectively solve?

What features could you add that would make your offer even more valuable to your customers?

How can you create the absolute best experience for those who have bought into what you're selling?

Asking customers for feedback is a way of being transparent and authentic with your customers. It shows them that you really care about them and their opinion and that you want to offer them the best possible product or service possible.

The more authentic you are with your customers, the more they'll support you over the long run. As they see how dedicated you are to constant improvement, they'll want to continue working with you and using your product or service.

PROVIDE AMAZING EXPERIENCES FOR YOUR CUSTOMERS

One of the best ways to get new customers and keep your existing customers is to create amazing experiences for them. These experiences don't need to be anything crazy. Your goal is to show them that you care deeply about them and want them to be incredibly happy with what you have to offer.

How can you create incredible experiences for your customers?

There are literally dozens of simple ways:

Provide amazing customer support

Send a handwritten thank you note with every product

Include an extra surprise with your product

Dedicate extended time to helping your clients work through their challenges

Send a card on the anniversary of their first purchase

Create short, custom videos thanking each one of your clients or customers

Call each customer just to say thank you

The list goes on and on. The goal is simply to make your customers feel special. You want them to feel like they really matter to you and aren't simply a way for you to make money.

The more you can delight and surprise your customers, the more likely it is that they'll tell their friends and colleagues about you, which will generate referral business. If you really go over the top with the way you treat your customers, you may even get exposure in prominent publications.

But ultimately, it's not about getting referral business or big exposure, although those things are certainly valuable. It's about treating your customers like real people who you actually care about.

THE ONLY THING WORSE THAN STARTING SOMETHING AND FAILING... IS NOT STARTING SOMETHING.

- SETH GODIN

BUILD SUSTAINABLE CASH FLOW

Eventually, if all things go well (and they will!), there will come a point where you have to decide whether or not you want to quit your day job and make your side hustle your full-time job.

Isn't that exciting to think about? You really could turn your passion project into a full-time, income producing job!

So how do you do that?

The final step is to get to the point where you have sustainable cash flow. In other words, you need to have a relatively stable amount of money coming in every month. If you have consistent cash flow, this gives you the option of quitting your day job.

How much sustainable cash flow should you have? Ideally, you want your side hustle to be generating at least 75% of your income. This will give you the flexibility to decide whether or not you want to quit your day job.

When thinking about your income, remember to take into account expenses. You'll have to pay self-employment tax at the end of the year. You also probably have expenses involved in keeping your side hustle up and running. Take all these things into account when deciding whether to make the plunge.

One important thing to note when it comes to quitting your day job. There will probably be a sense of fear and apprehension around quitting your job. After all, your job offers you stability.

Avoid allowing fear to keep you from following your dreams.

Fear is a big dream killer. If you've gotten your side hustle to the point where you're generating significant income, then it's time to seriously consider whether or not you should focus on doing it full time.

And consider this. If you're only doing your side hustle part time *and* you're making enough money to consider quitting your day job, think about how much more you could make if you were doing it full-time! Going full-time with your side hustle could actually produce significantly more income for you.

When that time comes, ask yourself, *"What is keeping me from taking the leap? What is keeping me from pursuing my dream full-time?"*

If the answer is fear, that might be a signal that it's actually time to go all-in on your side hustle.

I DON'T FOCUS ON WHAT I'M UP AGAINST. I FOCUS ON MY GOALS AND I TRY TO IGNORE THE REST.

- VENUS WILLIAMS

SIDE HUSTLE YOUR WAY TO FREEDOM

The beauty of the side hustle is that, when done properly, it can create freedom for you. If you're working a day job, it can give you additional income that can set you up for financial freedom. If you're not working a full-time job (like a stay-at-home mom), a side hustle can provide valuable income to your family.

And eventually, you may be able to take your passion and turn it into a full-time job. That's the real power of the side hustle!

Over the course of this book, you've learned a lot!

We talked about:

Preparing yourself for the hard work of the side hustle

Identifying your passions, desires, and skills

Validating your side hustle

Defining the goals that you want to achieve

Creating milestones that will keep your side hustle moving

Determining how you'll sell your side hustle products or services

Starting the actual process of selling

Marketing yourself effectively

Getting feedback from your customers

Providing amazing customer experiences

Building sustainable cash flow

You now know what you need to do in order to start making money with your side hustle. You even know what you need to do in order to transform your side hustle into a full-time job.

The only question now is, "What's stopping you?" Nothing is holding you back from getting your side hustle up and running.

So, don't wait any longer. Get hustling!

DAILY AFFIRMATIONS AND SELF REFLECTION TOOLS

BLESSINGS ARE REAL.

As I lift my eyes to the skies each morning, I see all the things that I am thankful for. They present themselves to me with ease once I am willing to come face to face with them.

The first thing I see is my family. Their faces beam down from the heavens with beautiful smiles.

Knowing their love and kindness fills my heart. I see their sincere wishes for me and I know that I am protected. I feel courageous enough to do scary things because I know that they believe in me.

I am also blessed with good health. I acknowledge all the things that my body is able to achieve on a daily basis.

When I look around and see others walking around with pain and discomfort, I immediately cease complaining. **I have so much to be thankful for.** I am able to do so many activities that contribute to my ongoing good health.

My job is such a blessing. Although I long for a higher paycheck, I am extremely grateful for the one that I have. It is more than many others have.

My earnings give me the opportunity to do many things and have many experiences. Those memories are like treasure forever stored in my mind.

Feeling blessed is a daily mindset that carries me through challenging times.

Today, I am so blessed. I lift up my eyes to the heavens and give thanks for all that my life contains today. Blessings bring so much to my life.

Self-Reflection Questions:

1. What are my three biggest blessings for the year so far?

2. How do I recognize a blessing in a difficult situation?

3. How do I convert a challenging event into a learning experience?

I AM FULL OF LIFE.

I embrace change. I accept transitions as natural. I welcome the opportunity to learn and grow. I focus on what I have to gain. I feel confident and resilient.

I try new things. I travel to different neighborhoods and foreign countries. I ask a friend to show me their favorite hobbies and sports. I experiment with gourmet recipes and exotic ingredients.

I pursue challenging goals. I give myself something to strive for each day. **I persevere through obstacles and enjoy the journey.**

I stay active. I exercise regularly and continue moving throughout the day. I take fitness classes or find a workout buddy to join me at the gym. I spend time outdoors running through the park and playing volleyball at the beach.

I do what I love. I practice my faith. I read inspirational texts and participate in my faith community. I think about the reason behind my actions. I feel motivated and fulfilled.

I connect with family and friends. I spend time hanging out with my loved ones. I plan fun parties and educational outings. I talk about my thoughts and feelings.

I make art. I express my creativity playing musical instruments or doing crafts with my kids.

I laugh out loud. I use gentle humor to help me through difficult situations. I watch cat videos and tell knock-knock jokes.

Today, I live with passion and purpose. **I feel hopeful and enthusiastic.** My life is rich and rewarding.

Self-Reflection Questions:

1. What makes me grateful to be alive?
2. What are some foods that give me more energy?
3. How does stress affect my energy levels?

I CHOOSE MY STATE OF BEING.

·············●··●●●●●·············

I am happy to know that I am in control of my reality.

Each morning, when I awake, I notice my state of being. I choose to wake up happy. I choose to be grateful for my good night's sleep. I give thanks for this warm bed and a safe home.

I am grateful for this new day.

When I start my day out with gratitude, my whole day goes more smoothly. I notice that nothing bothers me. I notice that there is a flow to traffic, and everyone is safe and in their own lane.

I notice that my interactions with others are easy and comfortable. I seem to flow through the day.

I enjoy the day - every day.

I start to notice even more enjoyable things. I see the blue sky. I feel the gentle breeze. I hear the laughter of children. I smell the flowers. I am enjoying my life.

I look for ways that I can help others enjoy their life more. I look for ways I can make people smile. I practice smiling with my eyes. I remember how to laugh.

I partake in activities that support my happy state of being. I take time to play with the dog. I take a moment to listen to my children. I sit and hold my partner's hand.

Today, I am grateful that I can create a happy state of being. I choose joy.

Self-Reflection Questions:

1. What behaviors can I do to create a happy state of being?
2. What thoughts shape my reality?
3. What emotions color my day?

I CHOOSE MY STATE OF BEING.

I am happy to know that I am in control of my reality.

Each morning, when I awake, I notice my state of being. I choose to wake up happy. I choose to be grateful for my good night's sleep. I give thanks for this warm bed and a safe home.

I am grateful for this new day.

When I start my day out with gratitude, my whole day goes more smoothly. I notice that nothing bothers me. I notice that there is a flow to traffic, and everyone is safe and in their own lane.

I notice that my interactions with others are easy and comfortable. I seem to flow through the day.

I enjoy the day - every day.

I start to notice even more enjoyable things. I see the blue sky. I feel the gentle breeze. I hear the laughter of children. I smell the flowers. I am enjoying my life.

I look for ways that I can help others enjoy their life more. I look for ways I can make people smile. I practice smiling with my eyes. I remember how to laugh.

I partake in activities that support my happy state of being. I take time to play with the dog. I take a moment to listen to my children. I sit and hold my partner's hand.

Today, I am grateful that I can create a happy state of being. I choose joy.

Self-Reflection Questions:

1. What behaviors can I do to create a happy state of being?

2. What thoughts shape my reality?

3. What emotions color my day?

MY LIFE JOURNEY BRINGS ME JOY.

Although I occasionally encounter tough times, at the end of the day, I still feel satisfaction, contentment, and pure happiness. Because I see life as an ever-changing journey, I approach each day with hopeful anticipation. I am filled with joy.

Each morning, I promise myself I can find at least one positive element in my day ahead. I notice the faces of people nearby. I cherish the sight of my family members. I am truly glad to see my co-workers. I am reminded of the incredible life I have.

The weather presents me with many reasons to feel joy. I admire a beautiful blue sky filled with puffy white clouds as I drive to work. The cleansing rain ensures that everything is green again. Even a blanket of snow gives me reason to smile.

My home, so simple yet so fit for me, welcomes me when I arrive.

My journey is predictable yet surprising, quiet yet vibrant, and calm yet fascinating. **I have joy because my life journey is a trip I look forward to taking each day.** Whatever path I take provides me with riches of happiness and satisfaction.

Today, I reflect on all the ways my life brings me joy and notice even the small pleasures that inevitably arise each day. I am blessed with a wonderful life journey.

Self-Reflection Questions:

1. How do I feel about the path my life is taking?
2. What joys have I encountered so far in this day?
3. Do I remind myself to stop and appreciate the joyful aspects of my life?

EACH DAY BRINGS JOY, FULFILLMENT, AND HAPPINESS.

Today is going to be a great day. I can just feel it. My expectations are so high that I can barely contain myself. A great day is definitely coming my way.

Feeling this way is becoming a habit for me. **When I expect to have a good day, I almost always do.** I have the power to shape my world with my expectations.

Today is the kind of day that makes me pleased to be alive. I feel joyful. I am thrilled just to be alive and experience today.

A great day also leaves me feeling fulfilled. **There is something satisfying about a good day that can be hard to describe, but I know I love experiencing it.** Today is one of those days.

Today, my happiness is overflowing. There are so many good things happening in my life. **I expect to feel joyful, fulfilled, and happy today.** Tomorrow is going to be even better.

Today, I am having the best day of my life. I expect each day to be the best I have ever had. Joy, fulfillment, and happiness are speeding in my direction. Today is a great day to be alive.

Self-Reflection Questions:

1. What is the best day I remember? What made it so great?
2. What can I do to have more great days?
3. Would I be more likely, or less likely, to have a great day if I expected to have a great day? Why?

I AM LIVING MY LIFE FULLY.

I am living my life fully now instead of waiting for some time in the future, like retirement, to enjoy my life.

I avoid waiting for circumstances outside of my control to change. I am living my life full out NOW!

I realize what is within my control. I can be anything I want to be. **I can do anything I want to do.** I can have anything I want to have. I know all of that is within my control.

I am choosing to live my life. I am taking the bull by the horns and riding that bull!

I am cashing in on all the things on my bucket list NOW!

I am taking the vacations that I always wanted to take. I realize that life is short. **I stop putting off my life and live it now!**

I am opening myself up to making new friends. I am opening myself up to new opportunities.

I am getting on that surfboard and feeling the exhilaration of living NOW!

I am kicking fear to the curb. I am DONE allowing fear to rule my life.

Today, I am doing things that I have always wanted to do but put off until tomorrow. I see now there is no tomorrow, only today.

Self-Reflection Questions:

1. What fears am I ready to eliminate now?
2. What stops me from going on vacation now?
3. What stops me from claiming my bucket list items now?

I CHOOSE TO BE CONTENT.

I realize that contentment is a choice. I am consciously choosing contentment in each moment.

In observing the neighborhood cats, I notice how they are content with what is. Regardless of the external circumstances, cats always land on their feet. I notice that they take naps when they can. I observe that cats go with the flow.

I am choosing to be like a cat. I am adopting their contentment with what is. I am taking naps when I am tired. I am flexible with what is. I adapt to my surroundings.

I love to observe a cat when it is curled up in front of a fireplace. I notice that the cat looks content. I am choosing to be a contented cat.

I am applying these observations into my life. I am taking time to play. **I am enjoying what is.**

I recognize that being content is a state of mind. I allow my mind to be content with what is. I allow my emotions to be fine with what is. I am finding contentment in my life.

Distractions fail to derail me. I catch myself quickly when my ego thinks it needs to be in control. I return to my contentment.

I am finding it easier each time I bring myself back to my contentment. I am retraining my brain. I am retraining my emotions. I am retraining my ego.

Today, I am grateful for what the stray cats are teaching me. I admire their confidence and individuality. I am smiling now like a contented kitty. I practice remaining in this state of contentment, even when distractions abound.

Self-Reflection Questions:

1. What can I do more of that will bring me into a state of contentment?

2. How can I release old patterns and be more content with what is?

3. What can I learn from cats that I want to apply to my life now?

I LIVE IN A LAND OF LIBERTY.

I recognize that I am very lucky to live in a land of liberty. I am so blessed. I am grateful for the many blessings that living in freedom brings to me. I am doing all I can to help others see how lucky they are as well.

I recognize that liberty starts within. I free up my mind to make space for liberty. **I realize that to free the mind is to be truly free.**

I eliminate any thoughts that limit my liberty. **I free my mind of limiting beliefs.** I let go of anything that is holding me back.

I liberate my thinking. I think outside the box. I free my mind.

I create a land of liberty inside my head. I use all my creative genius to construct my perfect world of freedom.

I do my part to help others free their minds from limiting beliefs too.

I value my liberty. I do what I can to influence the leaders of my community. I write to my congressman. I vote. I do my civic duty.

I preserve my liberty. I get more involved with community service. I participate in community activities.

I celebrate my liberty. I speak up at community gatherings. I write to the newspaper and get involved with projects that promote liberty.

Today, I am grateful that I can contribute to helping others and do my part to support freedom. Let freedom ring!

Self-Reflection Questions:

1. How can I contribute more fully to the liberty of my community?
2. How can I serve others to a greater extent?
3. Who could I help to find their liberty?

SHARING MAKES ME HAPPY.

I enjoy sharing my resources. Sharing fills my life with joy and meaning. My troubles seem less overwhelming when I focus on the needs of others. Sharing protects the environment and saves me money too.

Sharing strengthens my relationships. I earn trust and appreciation. I prevent conflicts by cooperating and taking turns.

Sharing builds my confidence and self-esteem. I feel valuable and powerful when I see how I can use my strengths and assets to help others. **I find satisfaction in having a positive impact on my world.**

I share tangible and intangible things. I provide money, food, and electric drills. I offer patience, empathy, and encouragement.

I support my family and friends. I divvy up household chores fairly with my partner and children. I reach out to relatives and friends who need emotional and material support during difficult times.

I lend a hand to my coworkers. I exchange constructive feedback and pass along interesting articles.

I do favors for my neighbors. I jump start their car or watch their home when they are out of town.

I perform random acts of kindness for strangers. I share a funny story or a sincere compliment.

Today, I connect with others by sharing my time, possessions, and skills. **The more I give to others, the more I receive.** Sharing makes me happier and more successful.

Self-Reflection Questions:

1. How do I balance sharing with others and taking care of my own needs?
2. How did my parents teach me to share?
3. What would the world be like without sharing?

EACH DAY I GROW MORE ENERGETIC AND VITAL.

Each day brings a new level of health and vitality. Though I am growing older, I am also growing better. My wisdom and perspective are a source of inspiration in my life.

I feel more powerful and energetic with each breath. Accordingly, my ability to withstand hardships and to persist also grows. I can withstand any challenge.

My optimism for life is a source of inspiration and vitality. It enables me to hold my head high and to claim my future with confidence and certainty. I adopt the most positive viewpoint in any situation. I guard my optimism as if it were made of gold.

I eliminate the things from my life that steal my energy or diminish my vitality. Anything that hampers me is eliminated. I place a premium on being my best. I feel lighter and freer when I drop the weight of negativity.

Maintaining healthy habits also refuels me. I eat nutritiously, exercise regularly, and sleep well.

The real secret of my energy and vitality is love. The love I receive and the love I give energize my soul. It is the fuel that powers me through the ups and downs of life. The more love that flows through my life, the more capable I become.

Today, I feel more capable than ever before. My vitality is at a maximum. I am overflowing with energy. I expect today to be one of my best.

Self-Reflection Questions:

1. What is the greatest source of inspiration in my life?
2. How can I strengthen my health?
3. What can I do to maximize my energy? How can I improve my diet, sleep, and exercise habits?

I AM LIVING MY PERFECT LIFE NOW.

·········•··•·•·········

This is the life I have been waiting for. This is living.

I realize that I have had the perfect life all along.

I am now aware that my perfect life has been here all the time. I no longer wait for the perfect life. My perfect life is here now.

With just that change in perspective, my life has changed. My life is now perfect. Simply because I am choosing to see it from that perspective. My life is perfect now. All is in perfection.

I realize now that with the statement of "I am waiting for…", I create a life of waiting for.

I stop waiting and start living!

I recognize in these tiny adjustments in thoughts and beliefs, I can totally transform my life. This is the life I have been waiting for because I have quit waiting for it. **I am living it!**

I see the perfection in all things.

I see the perfection in this "ah ha" moment. I have realized my perfect life! My perfect life is a reality! My perfect life has always been here, I just failed to see it that way before now.

I am amazed that I never saw this before. I am grateful that I see this now.

Today, I am grateful for my perfect life now!

Self-Reflection Questions:

1. What has shifted in my world, now that I see it as perfect?

2. What can I put in my journal about this perfect life?

3. How can I enjoy this perfection more fully?

I CHOOSE TO SMILE AND ENJOY LIFE TO THE FULLEST.

I can choose to be miserable, or I can choose to be happy: I choose to be happy. **Happiness is a choice that I make each day.** I choose to smile and to see the good in my life. I choose to see the good in the world.

I can choose to be bored, or I can choose to be enthusiastic: I choose to be enthusiastic about life. There are so many interesting things I can do, see, and learn.

I look forward to having an interesting day and experiencing something new. I am fascinated by everything the world has to offer.

I can be pessimistic, or I can be optimistic: I choose to be optimistic. I choose to smile at the possibilities each day has to offer. I expect something great to happen each day. I choose to live my life to the fullest.

I keep my eyes open for something to smile about. I easily find things to smile about several times throughout the day. The world is a magical place to me.

Today, I am smiling a big smile. **I am enjoying my life at the highest level and helping others to do the same.** Today is going to be a great day, and I am going to enjoy every minute of it.

Self-Reflection Questions:

1. What is something I could do regularly that would allow me to enjoy my life more?

2. What do I dread about each day? What changes can I make to make my life more pleasing to me?

3. What are the things that make me smile? Who are the people that make me smile?

I RECEIVE WHAT I NEED.

I am clear on what I desire. Knowing what I want is the critical first step to achieving it or acquiring it. I avoid relying on luck to achieve anything. **Once I know what I want, I do everything I can to ensure that I deserve it.**

When I put in the time and effort, the odds of success are infinitely greater.

I have accomplished, and continue to accomplish, many impressive things in my life. My history of success fills me with confidence and a positive attitude about the future. My past makes it clear that I can expect to receive everything I need in my life.

I believe in abundance and ensure that I give myself the best opportunity to experience it.

I have clarity of purpose. I know who I am and what I what. I work to achieve that purpose. I work so hard, and so consistently, that failure is a fluke. I deserve and receive what I need.

When I am clear on my goals and do the necessary work, magic happens. It is as if the universe is on my side. I am provided with everything I need.

Today, I purposefully pursue my goals. **I am consistent in my attitude and effort.** I earn everything I need, and I receive it.

Self-Reflection Questions:

1. What are the most important goals in my life right now?

2. What am I doing to achieve those goals? Do I deserve to be successful?

3. What is the biggest goal I have accomplished to date? How did I do it?

SIMPLE LIVING MAKES ME HAPPY.

L ess is more.

I slow down. I stop and take a few deep breaths when I am feeling rushed. I schedule breaks throughout the day. I use my vacation time.

I shorten my to-do list. I identify my top priorities. **I devote my time and energy to the activities that are meaningful to me.**

I clear away clutter. I sell or donate possessions that I rarely use. I keep my home and office tidy. I designate a place for each object and keep it there.

I work smarter. I do one thing at a time. I batch similar tasks together. I learn to delegate.

I create routines that remind me to live mindfully. I reflect and pray each morning and evening. I sit down to eat. I listen to my body. I spend time with my loved ones. **I focus on the present moment.**

I turn off my devices for at least an hour each day. I read before bed instead of watching TV. I put my phone away when I am driving or eating dinner with my family.

I consume less. **I value quality more than quantity.** I grow my own flowers and vegetables. I cook at home instead of ordering takeout. I walk or ride my bike to work. I shop less often and give myself time to think before making major purchases.

Today, I am content with what I have. I focus on the essentials. My life is simple and rewarding.

Self-Reflection Questions:

1. What am I teaching my children about simple living?
2. What are the advantages of traveling light?
3. How does simple living reduce daily stress?

EACH DAY IS A BLESSING AND A GIFT THAT I REFUSE TO WASTE.

There are only so many days in a lifetime. Life has an expiration date. Because I understand this fact, I avoid putting my life on hold.

Today is a great day to begin living my dreams. Why wait for the perfect day to put my plans into action? Today is as good a day as any. Today is the first day of the rest of my life.

I feel blessed to have another day on this great planet.

I can easily find beauty in my life. This alone is a great reason not to waste any time.

There is so much beauty to be seen. Nature, art, photographs, my friends and family, and all the other places I am able to appreciate the beauty are all around me.

I refuse to waste this day in any way, shape, or form. I have too much respect for life in general and my life in particular.

When I respect my time and my life, I naturally make the most of my day.

I am making the most of this day and ensuring that I go to bed with a smile on my face. There are few things better than knowing I had a great, productive day.

Today, I make the most of every minute. **Today is a gift that I am determined to squeeze every drop from.** Today is a blessing and a gift that I refuse to waste.

Self-Reflection Questions:

1. How much time do I waste each day? How do I waste time?

2. What could I accomplish if I reduced the amount of time I wasted?

3. What can I do today that will make my life better tomorrow?

I AM PEACEFUL, CALM, AND CONTENTED.

I relax easily. **Although many things in life are worth my attention, nothing is worth getting anxious or frustrated about.** All things happen in their own good time. Whatever comes to pass, I am peaceful, calm, and contented.

Inner peace is my birthright. I am pleased to be able to say that nothing truly rocks my boat. I handle all situations with the grace and ease that comes from being centered in myself.

In the face of challenges, I remain calm. I know that things usually work out for the better. New or challenging situations are inevitable parts of life, and I always make it through them just fine.

Contentment is also easy for me. I make time daily to remember all the things for which I am thankful, even if I do so just for a few moments as I drift off to sleep. This practice helps me stay happy with my own life, whatever comes.

If I ever find myself feeling upset or discontent, I ask myself what I really need right now. Is it some time to myself, alone?

Maybe I would feel nourished by a cup of hot tea, a warm bath, or the company of a good friend.

Whatever I need, I make it a priority to carve out time for it because I always feel calmer when my needs are met.

Today, I feel grounded and centered in myself. I am peaceful, calm, and contented. Each day, I consciously practice gratitude, which helps me maintain my inner balance.

Self-Reflection Questions:

4. When do I feel most peaceful?

5. Are there ways I can carry this feeling with me into other situations?

6. What is the relationship between gratitude and contentment?

I FEEL SAFE AND LOVED.

············ • • • • • • • • • • ············

My world is friendly and secure.

I appreciate myself as I am. I treat myself with compassion. I practice self-care. I eat healthy and exercise regularly. I speak to myself with kind and encouraging words. **I remember that I am worthy of love and respect.**

I develop mutually supportive relationships. I spend time with family and friends who give me constructive feedback and motivate me to pursue my goals. I enjoy deep conversations and fun nights out.

I maintain reasonable boundaries. I communicate tactfully and directly. I advocate for my needs. I let others know how I want to be treated.

I give generously. I share my time and resources. **Helping others makes me feel competent and connected.**

I embrace change. I recognize that transitions are a natural part of life. I keep my skills up to date. I welcome new opportunities with enthusiasm. I focus on what I have to gain.

I face reality. Trying to avoid conflicts and challenges can make me more anxious. I deal with situations head on. I give myself credit for trying. I teach myself that I am strong enough to handle what comes my way.

I count my blessings. **I pay attention to the times when others reward my trust and shower me with kindness.**

I reflect on my life and pray in gratitude. **I feel part of something bigger than myself.**

Today, I protect myself by making smart choices and turning to my loved ones when I need help. I am supported and safe.

Self-Reflection Questions:

1. How can establishing daily routines help me to feel more secure?
2. What does emotional safety mean to me?
3. How do I express my love?

I RETURN TO HAPPINESS.

Although this year has been very challenging, I choose to return to happiness. **I use many tools to aid me in my journey.**

I repeat affirmations to increase my happiness. Affirming my great qualities gives my confidence and self-esteem a much-needed boost.

Feeling thankful also returns me to happiness. Each day, I list ten things that I am grateful for. I am grateful for my gratitude journal.

One way to get me back to happiness that always works for me is to play. **I find new ways to play.** I play board games with my family. I chase the dog around the yard. I watch funny movies. I read jokes.

I think of memories of my youth that make me happy. I talk with my friends who have a great sense of humor. **I learn to cultivate my sense of humor.**

I love to watch funny animal antics on TV or the internet. I watch the squirrels chase each other in the yard.

I ask my friends and business associates what they do to increase their happiness. **I associate with happy people** and I adopt an attitude of happiness.

I remember the adage of the glass half full. I choose to see the world through rose colored glasses. I decorate my home with things that make me happy. **I find activities that bring me joy.**

Today, regardless of where I am or where I go, I can find happiness, because it is within.

Self-Reflection Questions:

1. What can I do right now to return to happiness?
2. How can I cultivate more happiness within?
3. Who can I call on right now that will make me laugh?

THIS IS EXACTLY WHERE I AM SUPPOSED TO BE.

••••••••●••••••••

Rarely are there days when I wish for things to be different. **I embrace what today offers my life.**

My job is difficult, but I take it one day at a time. I recognize the growth in my skills as a businessperson. In the midst of the challenging moments, **I maintain consciousness of the evolution that I am experiencing.**

Although my job is stressful, I know that it is preparing me to be successful in the next career venture that I undertake.

I maintain the same positive mindset when it comes to being single. The loneliness I experience today is an opportunity to learn to love myself unconditionally. **I believe that accepting myself prepares me to coexist with another person in love.**

Instead of feeling down about being alone, I use this time to discover new things about myself. It is wonderful to see myself blossoming.

Financial wellness is an ongoing target for me. Although it is sometimes difficult, I embrace the tough days when I have less in my pocket than desired. The challenging days are preparing me to handle wealth with humility and common sense.

I practice good financial habits when I have less so that I am able to appreciate and respect wealth when I have more.

Today, I pay keen attention to where I am in my life. I know that these twenty-four hours are a true blessing. **It is my responsibility and honor to be present in each moment** and extract the richness from my existence.

Self-Reflection Questions:

1. What steps can I take to get myself from here to the next phase in my career?

2. What do I do to get the most out of my downtime after work?

3. How do I evaluate whether an opportunity is right for me?

EXPLORING THE WORLD IS EXCITING.

When I take the time to explore the world, a sense of excitement builds within me. It makes me happy to see the beauty that exists in so much of the world.

I get excited because I know that something new is on the horizon. Being open to exploring creates opportunities for me to expand my knowledge and experience.

When I visit a new country, I eagerly anticipate learning more about the culture. I am respectful of the differences between people. I am thrilled to discover them.

There are things that surprise me everywhere I turn. The origins of a language or the special way a meal is prepared create a sense of amazement. I feel like a child again when I set off on a new adventure of exploration.

Learning a new language is stimulating. Being able to communicate gives me the chance to meet new friends and colleagues.

Studying history gives me a greater appreciation of life in the present. I enjoy learning about where native people are coming from. **It is humbling to discover the richness in the stories of ancestors in different parts of the world.**

It is a good feeling to introduce others to my newfound knowledge, too, with stories of my adventures.

Today, I am a happy wanderer who relishes each opportunity to visit somewhere new. It is my mission to bring the world closer together by sharing my knowledge with as many people as possible.

Self-Reflection Questions:

1. What are the benefits of exploring a new country on my own?

2. What are the important things to take with me on an exploration?

3. How do I make my discoveries known to others?

I AM SO HAPPY.

My life is meaningful and joyful. **I develop close relationships that are healthy and mutually supportive.** I cherish my family and friends. I block out time for my loved ones. I am proactive about scheduling family dinners and weekend outings. I feel understood and cared for.

I make choices that reflect my values. I stand up for my principles.

I slow down. I live mindfully. I focus on the present. I notice the small miracles that happen each day. **I savor little pleasures and create beautiful memories.**

I balance my work and personal life. I set realistic expectations. I manage my time efficiently. I learn to prioritize and delegate.

I use my strengths and follow my passions. I work on my communication skills and increase my emotional intelligence. I fill my leisure time with rewarding hobbies and activities. I grow vegetables and play musical instruments.

I appreciate nature. I spend time outdoors. I play sports and walk around green spaces. I listen to birds sing and smell the fresh air.

I laugh and play. I share jokes and funny stories. I watch comedies and cat videos. I stage puppet shows with my children and make a game out of household chores.

I help others. I support worthy causes and give back to my community. I volunteer my time and services. I take pleasure in making my neighborhood more vibrant and inclusive.

Today, I am peaceful and content. My world is friendly and warm. My happiness comes from within.

Self-Reflection Questions:

1. What would I tell my childhood self about how to be happy?
2. Is happiness more like a journey or a destination?
3. How does technology affect my happiness?

I FIND HAPPINESS IN THE PRESENT.

M y happiness is in the here and now. I cultivate mindfulness and contentment.

I slow down. I take deep breaths that calm my body and mind. I pay attention to my surroundings.

I count my blessings. I give thanks for my family and friends. I appreciate having a healthy body and a strong mind.

I perform one task at a time. I maximize my productivity by focusing on what I am doing now. I think about my purpose when I am washing dishes or serving others. **Each activity becomes more meaningful and memorable.**

I face challenges head on. I deal with conflicts and setbacks instead of letting anxiety build up.

I accept uncertainty. I am confident that I can handle changes in my relationships and career. **I welcome the opportunity to learn and grow.**

I reach out to others. I feel closer to my loved ones when I am fully engaged in having a conversation or playing a board game.

Even strangers seem more interesting and friendlier when I care about their wellbeing.

I savor my food. Even a simple snack becomes more satisfying when I arrange it carefully and take small bites.

Today, I pay attention to the present and enjoy the happiness that it contains. I choose to live in the moment.

Self-Reflection Questions:

1. How does mindfulness contribute to happiness?
2. What is one thing I can do to sharpen my awareness?
3. How can daily meditation help me to connect with the present?

I SEE ALL THE BLESSINGS AROUND ME.

I start from the moment I awake. I am grateful for the sunshine that gently arouses me from my slumber. **I am grateful for the birds who bring forth the dawn.**

I am grateful for water to splash my face awake and toothpaste to freshen my mouth. I am blessed to have modern conveniences that make my life pleasant.

I am blessed to have food in the house. I am blessed to have shelter and plenty of clothing. I am thankful for shoes and socks.

I am blessed to have reliable transportation, a phone to communicate with, and a computer with which to do my work.

I am blessed to have an office, wonderful workmates, and amazing clients.

I am blessed to have a wonderful family, fantastic friends, and reliable neighbors.

I am blessed to have a fur baby. I am grateful for all the pets I have had in my life. I have wonderful memories of all my furry friends.

I am grateful that I have plenty of money to take care of my needs.

I find that the more I bless others with kindness, the more blessings I receive as well.

Today and every day, I find more things to be thankful for. **I am thankful for the abundance in my life.** I am truly blessed beyond measure.

Self-Reflection Questions:

1. How can I be a blessing to more people in my life?
2. What acts of kindness can I show my loved ones?
3. How can I be a greater blessing to the world?

TODAY IS A DAY OF HAPPINESS AND PEACE FOR ME.

I am choosing to find happiness in my life today. I have many things to be thankful and happy about.

When I consider my many blessings, I feel happy and at peace. **I am fortunate to have a life that I enjoy so much.**

I have many wonderful friends that support me and add joy to my life.

I am emotionally supported by the important people in my life. There are people that support me at my workplace. My neighbors are kind and helpful. **My friends and family are always there for me.**

Knowing that I have so much support in life brings a feeling of constant peace.

I am content with my life. **I have everything I truly need,** or I have the means to acquire them. I want for nothing, so I am at peace.

I have a high level of emotional comfort. My mind is relaxed. My body is relaxed. My soul is at peace.

Today, I am looking forward to a happy and peaceful day. **I am releasing everything from my life that stands in the way of happiness and peace.** I am committed to living my best life. Today is a day of happiness and peace for me.

Self-Reflection Questions:

1. When do I feel the most peaceful? When do I feel the least peaceful? Why?
2. When do I feel the happiest? When do I feel the least happy? Why?
3. What are the changes I can make in my life that will result in greater levels of happiness and peacefulness? What would change if I were happier and enjoyed a higher level of peace?

HAPPINESS HEALS ME.

............●●●●●●●●...

A positive attitude supports my mental and physical wellbeing. Happiness is healing.

Being cheerful gives me the motivation and energy to take care of myself. I adopt lifestyle habits that keep me strong and fit.

I stay active and exercise regularly. I strengthen my heart and muscles. I increase my flexibility and balance. I take breaks from sitting. I do manual chores and more around more each day.

I eat a nutritious diet. I prepare delicious meals and snacks with vegetables, fruits, and other whole foods. I cut back on added sugar and salt.

I manage my weight. I lose excess pounds safely and gradually.

I sleep well. I stick to a consistent schedule for going to bed and waking up. I use soothing rituals that help me to fall asleep quickly. I keep my bedroom dark and quiet.

I reduce stress. I find something to laugh about in difficult situations. **I let minor annoyances slide off my back instead of dwelling on them.** I find relaxation practices that work for me.

I stay connected. I cultivate close relationships. I express gratitude and affection. I stay in touch with family and friends. I ask for help when I need it.

I set goals. I challenge myself to keep growing and learning.

I talk with my doctor. I discuss my mental health as well as physical symptoms. I ask questions and follow their recommendations.

Today, I lead a happy and healthy life. I invest in myself by being positive and purposeful.

Self-Reflection Questions:

1. How do I define happiness?
2. What is the difference between happiness and pleasure?
3. How do my emotions affect my health?

I FIND THE SWEETNESS IN LIFE.

J ust as the bear finds honey hidden in a tree, I find the sweetness hidden in life.

Sometimes the sweetness isn't evident. **I have to look for it.** It may be tucked away in odd places. I awaken my "spidey sense" to notice the tiny surprises each day.

I spot a shiny penny on the ground that wants to come home in my pocket. I take that as a sign that money is coming my way. I am grateful that I listen to my intuition and look on the ground at the perfect moment.

A feather lightly touches the ground just in front of me, and I pick it up to give to my friend who collects feathers. I love to find random objects that remind me of my sweet friends. I find the perfect moment to surprise them with a simple gift from the heart. I enjoy seeing their delight as they open their surprise gift from the heart.

I find that a walk on the beach produces many gifts from the sea that I can share with others. I always tell the ocean thank you. I say a little prayer for all the sea creatures.

My heart fills with gratitude for the beauty and bounty that I find all around me.

I make a game out of finding the sweetness of life. Just taking the time to smell the freshness of the breeze fills my heart with gladness. I feel the sun on my skin and am grateful for the light and warmth of the sun. Thank you, Sunshine!

Today, I take the time to see, hear, smell, taste, and touch the sweetness of this Wonderful World. I notice acts of kindness. I pass on the sweetness to others. I am uplifted each and every day by the sweetness of life.

Self-Reflection Questions:

1. What scenarios in my life remind me how sweet life is?
2. How can I conjure up more joy from life?
3. Who brings sweetness to my life?

I START EACH DAY FEELING HAPPY AND ENTHUSIASTIC.

·············●·········

I make the decision to start each day with a bang. I know that having a positive and enthusiastic attitude each morning helps to guarantee that a great day is on the agenda.

I have a good day when I have a good morning. My morning attitude is under my control, so I choose to have a positive mental attitude.

I make a plan for my day that is productive and creates enthusiasm. I feel excited when I think about how much I am going to accomplish during the day.

Each day is a gift that I pledge to make the most of.

I love life, and my life brings me joy.

Each morning, I visualize having an amazing day. This supercharges my positive feelings, and I create a great attitude in myself. **I am always optimistic about my day.** I look forward to seeing what the day brings.

I feel gratitude each day. Before I get out of bed, I make a mental list of everything that makes me feel thankful. I have every reason to feel happy when I feel grateful.

Today, I am starting my day with happiness and enthusiasm. **I am looking forward to having a joyful and productive day.** My positive feelings are rubbing off on everyone around me.

Self-Reflection Questions:

1. What is my morning routine? What changes could I make to my morning routine to feel more happiness and enthusiasm at the start of my day?

2. How would my results change if I started the day happy and enthusiastic?

3. How is the quality of my day affected by my morning attitude?

TODAY IS AN AMAZING DAY.

Today is a great day. I am free from the past because I only focus on Today. By focusing on today, I allow great things to happen. I live one day at a time.

I count my blessing each day and am grateful for the opportunity to live another day. My life is a gift and I am grateful.

I greet each day with high expectations and a child-like wonder. I smile before getting out of bed each morning. I know good things are going to happen. High expectations bring exceptional results into my life. I receive what I expect.

Occasionally, I may have a day that provides challenges, but I maintain a positive attitude. I know that I can handle any challenge with ease and with a smile on my face.

I only expect the best to happen but I am prepared for anything.

The choices I make today ensure that my day is exciting and interesting. I am free of negative expectations and doubt.

I know that the quality of my thoughts determines the quality of my day, so I maintain positive thoughts.

Today, I choose to have another great day. I choose to expect the best from those around me and myself. I rise above my past and expect a bright future. Today is an amazing day.

Self-Reflection Questions:

1. What was the best thing that happened today?
2. What do I need to remove from my live to ensure my average day improves?
3. What would make today great?

HAPPINESS IS A HABIT.

I make choices that bring me inner peace and joy. I create routines that make my life harmonious and satisfying.

I treat myself with compassion. I love and accept myself as I am. I use positive self-talk. I practice self-care and adopt a growth mindset. I learn from experience. I forgive myself and move on.

I give generously. I share my time, talents, and resources with others. **I take pleasure in seeing others smile.**

I develop mutually supportive relationships. I allow myself to be vulnerable. I talk about my thoughts and feelings. I ask for help when I am struggling.

I manage stress. **I live mindfully.** I find relaxation practices that work for me. I breathe deeply and meditate. I listen to instrumental music or take a walk in the park. I think positive and repeat affirmations.

I cultivate gratitude. I remember the many things I am thankful for. I tell others how much they mean to me.

I do meaningful work and fill my leisure time with rewarding activities. My confidence grows when I see myself having a positive impact.

I laugh and play. Humor lifts my spirits. It promotes healing and draws me closer to others. I run around with my children. I watch cat videos. I turn difficult situations into funny stories that I can talk about at dinner.

Today, I enjoy tranquility and bliss. My habits make my life more peaceful and happier.

Self-Reflection Questions:

1. Why is happiness more like a path than a destination?

2. Why does cheering someone up make me feel happy too?

3. How can simple living make me happier?

I FULFILL MY RESPONSIBILITIES WITH JOY.

I consider myself blessed to be able to perform all of my tasks. I am grateful for the energy and resources at my disposal, which enable me to do my work well in all areas of my life.

Instead of feeling sorry for myself for having so many responsibilities, I think of myself as fortunate to have the opportunity to be active. **Being needed makes me feel important.**

I fulfill my responsibilities with joy because I've come to the place of understanding that these are actually privileges. I've been chosen and equipped to perform purposeful work. What I do makes a difference in the lives of others.

When I look at my responsibilities as privileges, I am able to see the value within me. I am worth more than I will ever know. There are people and places benefiting from what I do without me even knowing about it.

Every time I put my hand to work, I am shaping history. My work is valuable even when it seems tedious. No matter what I am involved in, my work is meaningful.

I erase complaints from my vocabulary. Negativity is absent from my speech because its only outcome is bitterness. **I replace negativity with a happy heart so I can enjoy my work and also perform better.**

I infuse my work with joy by singing or smiling throughout my day. I decorate my workspace with photos of my loved ones' smiling faces to remind myself of the reasons why I work.

Today, I choose to fulfill my responsibilities with a positive attitude and a grateful heart. I overflow with joy when I think about the privilege I have to touch others through my work.

Self-Reflection Questions:

1. What attitude have I been expressing toward my responsibilities?
2. How does a joyful attitude improve my morale and overall performance?
3. How can I infuse joy into my work?

Made in the USA
Columbia, SC
03 July 2023